The Anatomy of a Money Crunch;

Understanding the Factors That Lead to Financial Crisis in a Country

By

Ruth R. Hamilton

Table of contents

Chapter 1

Definition of a money crunch

A money crunch, also known as a financial crunch, refers to a situation where there is a shortage of cash or liquidity in an economy or a particular market. This can occur when there is a sudden decrease in the supply of money or credit, or an increase in the demand for money or credit, resulting in a tight financial situation. A money crunch can lead to a range of economic problems, including a recession, high inflation, or a financial crisis. It can also affect individuals, businesses, and governments who may struggle to pay their debts or access credit.

Importance of understanding the causes of a money crunch

Understanding the causes of a money crunch is crucial because it helps individuals, businesses, and policymakers to take necessary measures to prevent or mitigate its impact. Here are some key reasons why understanding the causes of a money crunch is important:

Preventing economic instability: A money crunch can lead to economic instability, including recession, high inflation, or even a financial crisis. By understanding the causes of a money crunch, policymakers can take necessary measures to prevent or mitigate the impact of such situations on the economy.

Managing risks: Businesses and individuals can be impacted by a money crunch if they are unable to pay their debts or access credit. Understanding the causes of a money crunch helps them to identify potential risks and take measures to manage them.

Planning for the future: By understanding the causes of a money crunch, policymakers and businesses can plan for the future, such as implementing policies that promote financial stability or adjusting business strategies to minimize financial risks.

Protecting investments: Investors need to be aware of the causes of a money crunch to protect their investments. This includes diversifying their portfolios, monitoring economic indicators, and adjusting their investment strategies accordingly.

Overall, understanding the causes of a money crunch is essential for maintaining financial stability, managing risks, and planning for the future.

Chapter 2

Macroeconomic Factors.

Macroeconomic factors refer to the large-scale economic variables that affect an entire economy or a significant portion of it. These factors can have a significant impact on businesses, governments, and individuals.

Some of the most important macroeconomic factors include:

Gross Domestic Product (GDP): GDP is a measure of the total value of goods and services produced within an economy over a given period. It is a key indicator of economic growth and is often used to compare the economic performance of different countries.

Inflation: Inflation refers to the rate at which the general level of prices for goods and services is rising over time. It is an important factor to monitor, as high inflation can erode the purchasing power of consumers and lead to economic instability.

Unemployment: Unemployment is the percentage of people in the labor force who are not currently employed but are actively seeking work. High unemployment rates can indicate economic weakness, while low unemployment rates can indicate a strong economy.

Interest rates: Interest rates are the cost of borrowing money and are set by central banks. High interest rates can discourage borrowing and investment, while low interest rates can stimulate economic activity.

Trade balance: The trade balance is the difference between a country's exports and imports. A trade surplus occurs when a country exports more than it imports, while a trade deficit occurs when a country imports more than it exports. Trade imbalances can affect currency values and can have implications for domestic businesses and consumers.

Government policies: Government policies, such as fiscal and monetary policies, can have a significant impact on the economy. For example, government spending and taxation can affect economic growth and inflation, while central bank policies can affect interest rates and the money supply.

Inflation

Inflation refers to the general increase in the price level of goods and services in an economy over time. It is often measured as the percentage change in the Consumer Price Index (CPI), which tracks the prices of a basket of goods and services that consumers typically purchase.

Inflation can be caused by a variety of factors, such as an increase in demand for goods and services, a decrease in the supply of goods and services, or an increase in the money supply. When there is more demand for goods and services than there is supply, prices tend to go up. Similarly, when the supply of money in an economy increases, the prices of goods and services also tend to increase, as there is more money chasing the same amount of goods and services.

Inflation is generally considered to be a negative phenomenon because it erodes the purchasing power of money over time. When prices are rising, the same amount of money can buy fewer goods and services, which can lead to a decline in living standards for people on fixed incomes or with limited financial resources. It can also lead to uncertainty and volatility in financial markets, as investors and businesses try to anticipate future inflation rates and adjust their strategies accordingly.

Interest rates: refer to the cost of borrowing money or the return on lending money. When someone borrows money, they typically have to pay interest on the loan, which is a percentage of the amount borrowed. Similarly, when someone lends money, they earn interest on the loan, which is a percentage of the amount lent. Interest rates are set by central banks or other financial institutions and can have a significant impact on the economy. For example, when interest rates are low, borrowing becomes cheaper and more people are likely to take out loans, which can stimulate economic growth. On the other hand, when interest rates are high, borrowing becomes more expensive and people may be less likely to take out loans, which can slow down economic activity.

Exchange rates refer to the value of one currency in relation to another currency. For example, the exchange rate between the US dollar and the euro determines how many euros someone can get in exchange for one US dollar. Exchange rates are determined by supply and demand in foreign exchange markets and can be affected by a variety of factors, such as economic conditions, political events, and interest rates. When a currency appreciates, it becomes more valuable relative to other currencies, which can make exports more expensive and imports cheaper. Conversely, when a currency depreciates, it becomes less valuable relative to other currencies, which can make exports cheaper and imports more expensive. Exchange rates can have a significant impact on international trade and investment, as well as on the profitability of multinational corporations.

Government dept:

Government debt refers to the amount of money that a government owes to lenders, such as individuals, institutions, or other governments. It is usually expressed as a percentage of a country's Gross Domestic Product (GDP), which is the total value of all goods and services produced within a country in a given period of time.

Governments often borrow money by issuing bonds, which are debt securities that pay interest to investors over a set period of time. The money raised from the sale of these bonds is typically used to finance government spending, such as infrastructure projects, social programs, or national defense.

While government debt can help finance important investments and programs, high levels of debt can also have negative consequences. For example, if a government has to spend a significant portion of its budget on debt payments, it may have less money available to invest in other areas, such as education or healthcare. High levels of debt can also lead to higher interest rates and inflation, which can make it more difficult for businesses and individuals to borrow money and invest in the economy.

Governments can reduce their debt levels by increasing taxes, reducing spending, or increasing economic growth. However, these measures can be politically difficult to implement and can have their own economic and social consequences. As such, managing government debt is a complex issue that requires balancing the need for investment and growth with the need for fiscal responsibility.

Fiscal policy:

Fiscal policy refers to the government's use of taxation, spending, and borrowing to influence the economy. It is one of the two main tools used by governments to stabilize and manage the economy, the other being monetary policy.

Fiscal policy can be expansionary or contractionary. Expansionary fiscal policy involves increasing government spending or cutting taxes to stimulate economic growth and reduce unemployment. This can lead to higher inflation if the economy is already operating at full capacity. Conversely, contractionary fiscal policy involves reducing government spending or increasing taxes to slow down economic growth and combat inflation.

Fiscal policy is a powerful tool that can have significant effects on the economy. However, its effectiveness depends on several factors, including the state of the economy, the magnitude and timing of policy changes, and the government's ability to implement them effectively.

Monetary policy:

Monetary policy refers to the actions taken by a central bank, such as the Federal Reserve in the United States, to regulate the supply of money and credit in the economy. The goal of monetary policy is to promote economic stability and growth by influencing interest rates, controlling inflation, and ensuring the availability of credit.

Central banks use a range of tools to implement monetary policy, including adjusting the reserve requirement for banks, buying and selling government securities, and setting short-term interest rates. When the central bank lowers interest rates, it encourages borrowing and spending, which can stimulate economic growth. Conversely, when it raises interest rates, it can slow down borrowing and spending, which can help to control inflation.

The effectiveness of monetary policy depends on various factors, including the strength of the economy, the nature of the financial system, and the behavior of consumers and businesses. In addition, the impact of monetary policy can take time to materialize, which is why central banks often use a gradual approach when making policy changes.

Chapter 3

External Factors

External factors are elements outside of an individual, organization, or system that can influence its operations or outcomes. These factors can be economic, social, political, technological, environmental, or legal in nature, among others. They are typically beyond the control of the entity being affected, but can have a significant impact on its performance.

Examples of external factors include changes in consumer preferences, shifts in market trends, fluctuations in currency exchange rates, changes in government policies or regulations, natural disasters, technological advancements, and competitive pressures.

Understanding external factors is important for businesses and organizations as they can affect their ability to achieve their goals and objectives. By analyzing these factors and incorporating them into their strategic planning, businesses can better position themselves to adapt to changes and take advantage of opportunities that arise.

Trade imbalances:

Trade imbalances refer to situations where the value of a country's imports exceeds its exports, or vice versa. This can create economic imbalances between countries and can have an impact on exchange rates and international trade. Trade imbalances can occur due to a variety of factors, including differences in production costs, exchange rates, and government policies.

Capital flight: refers to the movement of assets or capital out of a country. This can occur when individuals or companies lose confidence in the economic or political stability of a country, and seek to move their assets to other countries with more favorable conditions. Capital flight can have negative impacts on the economy of the country experiencing it, as it can lead to a decrease in investment, lower economic growth, and currency devaluation.

Both trade imbalances and capital flight are important considerations in international economics and finance, and policymakers often work to address these issues through a variety of measures, such as trade agreements, exchange rate policies, and capital controls.

Foreign investment:

Foreign investment refers to the investment made by individuals, companies, or governments from one country into another country. This can take various forms, including direct investment, portfolio investment, and foreign aid.

Direct investment involves the establishment of a business or acquisition of a stake in an existing business in another country, with the aim of controlling or influencing its operations. Portfolio investment, on the other hand, involves investing in financial assets such as stocks, bonds, or mutual funds in a foreign country.

Foreign investment can bring various benefits to the host country, such as increased capital, job creation, technology transfer, and improved infrastructure. It can also lead to increased competition and productivity, as well as access to new markets and expertise.

However, foreign investment can also have potential drawbacks, such as the risk of loss of control over key industries or assets, environmental concerns, and the potential for negative impacts on local communities.

Governments often seek to attract foreign investment through policies such as tax incentives, streamlined regulatory processes, and investment guarantees. At the same time, they also seek to balance the benefits of foreign investment with potential risks and negative impacts on their economies and societies.

Natural disasters and other external shocks:

Natural disasters and other external shocks refer to unexpected events or circumstances that can have a significant impact on economies, businesses, and societies. These events can include natural disasters such as earthquakes, hurricanes, floods, or droughts, as well as geopolitical events such as wars, terrorism, or economic sanctions.

The impact of these external shocks can vary depending on the severity and duration of the event, as well as the preparedness of the affected area. Natural disasters can cause significant physical damage to infrastructure, disrupt supply chains, and lead to loss of life and displacement of people. Geopolitical events can disrupt trade and investment flows, destabilize governments, and cause social and economic unrest.

The economic consequences of external shocks can include reduced productivity, decreased investment, higher inflation, and increased unemployment. In extreme cases, external shocks can lead to economic recession or even depression.

To mitigate the impact of external shocks, governments and businesses can take various measures. These may include disaster preparedness planning, diversification of supply chains and investments, emergency response mechanisms, and financial assistance programs. In some cases, international cooperation and aid may also be necessary to address the impact of external shocks.

Chapter 4

Internal Factors

Internal factors refer to the characteristics and elements that are found within an organization and can affect its performance, growth, and success. These factors are generally under the control of the organization and can be modified or changed to improve its performance. Here are some examples of internal factors:

Leadership: The quality of leadership within an organization can have a significant impact on its success. Good leaders can inspire and motivate employees to perform their best, while poor leadership can lead to low morale and a lack of direction.

Corporate culture: The values, beliefs, and practices that make up an organization's culture can have a major influence on its performance. A strong, positive culture can foster teamwork, creativity, and innovation, while a negative or toxic culture can stifle growth and lead to high turnover.

Human resources: The quality and skill level of an organization's employees can have a significant impact on its performance. Investing in employee training and development, recruiting top talent, and retaining key employees can all contribute to a company's success.

Financial resources: The financial resources available to an organization can also play a key role in its success. A company with strong financial backing may have more resources to invest in growth opportunities, while a company with limited resources may struggle to compete.

Technology and infrastructure: The technology and infrastructure used by an organization can also impact its performance. An outdated or inefficient system can slow down operations, while modern technology and infrastructure can improve efficiency and productivity.

Marketing and branding: An organization's marketing and branding efforts can also affect its success. A strong brand identity and effective marketing campaigns can help to attract customers and build loyalty, while poor marketing can hinder growth and lead to decreased sales.

Corruption and political instability:

Corruption and political instability are two external factors that can have a significant impact on the performance and success of businesses and organizations operating within a country or region.

Corruption refers to the abuse of power or position for personal gain. When corruption is prevalent, it can make it difficult for businesses to operate fairly and transparently. Bribery, kickbacks, and other corrupt practices can create a culture of dishonesty that can undermine the rule of law and discourage investment. Companies may find it difficult to obtain necessary permits or licenses, or to compete for contracts, if they are not willing to engage in corrupt practices. In addition, corruption can raise the cost of doing business, as companies may need to pay bribes or make other concessions to operate.

Political instability can also have a significant impact on businesses. When there is political unrest or uncertainty, it can lead to economic instability, which can make it difficult for businesses to plan for the future. Changes in government policies or leadership can create uncertainty and unpredictability, which can be challenging for companies to navigate. In extreme cases, political instability can lead to civil unrest, violence, or even war, which can have devastating consequences for businesses and communities.

Overall, corruption and political instability can create an environment that is unfavorable for business. Companies may find it difficult to operate efficiently, attract investment, or plan for the future when these factors are present. It is important for businesses to be aware of these external factors and to take steps to mitigate their impact, such as investing in robust compliance programs or diversifying their operations across multiple regions.

Mismanagement of public finances:

Mismanagement of public finances refers to the improper or irresponsible use of public funds by government officials. This can occur when funds are misused, embezzled, or diverted for personal gain, or when they are not used effectively to benefit citizens or achieve public policy goals.

The impact of mismanagement of public finances on businesses and organizations can be significant. Here are some of the ways in which it can affect the business environment:

Reduced government spending: When public funds are mismanaged, governments may be forced to reduce spending in areas that are important to businesses, such as infrastructure, education, or healthcare. This can lead to a decline in the quality of services, which can in turn impact the business environment.

Limited investment: Mismanagement of public finances can also discourage private investment, as investors may be wary of putting their money into an environment where corruption and inefficiency are prevalent. This can lead to a lack of investment in key sectors, such as energy, transportation, or telecommunications.

Unfair competition: When public funds are misused, it can create unfair competition for businesses that operate within the rules. For example, if government contracts are awarded based on personal connections rather than merit, businesses that are not connected may struggle to compete.

Weakened economic growth: Mismanagement of public finances can also lead to weakened economic growth, as funds that could be used to stimulate the economy are diverted or misused. This can result in higher taxes, lower wages, and reduced consumer spending.

Mismanagement of public finances can create an uncertain and challenging business environment. It is important for businesses to be aware of the risks associated with corruption and inefficiency in government, and to advocate for transparent and accountable governance practices.

Poor infrastructure and education:

Poor infrastructure and education are two external factors that can have a significant impact on businesses and organizations. Here's how:

Poor infrastructure:

Infrastructure refers to the physical structures and systems that support economic activity, such as transportation networks, communication systems, and energy grids. When infrastructure is inadequate, it can create challenges for businesses in several ways:

Limited access to markets: Poor infrastructure can limit access to markets, making it difficult for businesses to transport goods or reach customers in remote areas.

Increased costs: Inadequate infrastructure can also increase costs for businesses, as they may need to invest in their own infrastructure or use more expensive transportation options.

Reduced productivity: Poor infrastructure can also reduce productivity, as employees may spend more time commuting or waiting for goods to be delivered.

Poor education:

Education refers to the knowledge and skills that individuals acquire through formal or informal learning. When education is inadequate, it can create challenges for businesses in several ways:

Limited pool of talent: Poor education can limit the pool of talent available to businesses, as individuals may not have the skills or knowledge necessary to perform certain jobs.

Reduced innovation: Inadequate education can also reduce innovation, as individuals may lack the knowledge or training to develop new ideas or technologies.

Reduced competitiveness: Poor education can also reduce a country's competitiveness, as businesses may struggle to compete with others that have better-educated workforces.

Poor infrastructure and education can create an environment that is challenging for businesses. It is important for governments to invest in these areas to support economic growth and development, and for businesses to advocate for policies that promote infrastructure development and education.

Income inequality and poverty: Income inequality and poverty are two external factors that can have a significant impact on businesses and organizations. Here's how:

Income inequality:

Income inequality refers to the unequal distribution of income across different groups of people in a society. When income inequality is high, it can create challenges for businesses in several ways:

Reduced consumer demand: High income inequality can reduce consumer demand for goods and services, as those with lower incomes may not have the resources to purchase them.

Limited talent pool: High income inequality can also limit the pool of talent available to businesses, as individuals from lower-income backgrounds may not have had access to the education and training necessary to perform certain jobs.

Social unrest: High income inequality can also lead to social unrest, as those with lower incomes may feel that the system is rigged against them. This can create a challenging business environment, as companies may be targets of protests or other forms of civil unrest.

Poverty:

Poverty refers to a lack of access to basic needs, such as food, shelter, and healthcare. When poverty is high, it can create challenges for businesses in several ways:

Reduced consumer demand: Like income inequality, poverty can reduce consumer demand for goods and services, as those living in poverty may not have the resources to purchase them.

Reduced workforce productivity: Poverty can also reduce workforce productivity, as individuals living in poverty may be more likely to experience health problems or have difficulty accessing education and training.

Increased social costs: Poverty can also lead to increased social costs, such as crime and healthcare costs. This can create a challenging business environment, as companies may be required to bear some of these costs.

Income inequality and poverty can create an environment that is challenging for businesses. It is important for governments to address these issues to support economic growth and development, and for businesses to advocate for policies that promote equality and reduce poverty.

Demographic trends:

Demographic trends refer to changes in the size, composition, and distribution of populations over time. These trends can have a significant impact on businesses and organizations in several ways:

Changing consumer demand: Demographic trends can impact consumer demand, as different age groups and demographic segments may have different needs and preferences. For example, an aging population may create increased demand for healthcare and retirement services.

Workforce composition: Demographic trends can also impact the composition of the workforce, as different age groups and demographic segments may have different skills and experience. For example, a growing population of young people may provide opportunities for businesses to tap into new talent pools.

Geographic distribution: Demographic trends can impact the geographic distribution of populations, which can in turn impact the location and growth of businesses. For example, a trend towards urbanization may create opportunities for businesses that operate in cities, while those that operate in rural areas may face challenges.

Diversity and inclusion: Demographic trends can also impact diversity and inclusion in the workplace, as different demographic segments may have different experiences and perspectives. Businesses that are able to effectively leverage diversity and create an inclusive workplace may be better positioned to succeed in the long term.

Businesses that are able to anticipate and adapt to demographic trends may be better positioned to succeed in the long term. It is important for businesses to pay attention to demographic changes and adjust their strategies accordingly, whether that means adapting to changing consumer demands, tapping into new talent pools, or creating a more diverse and inclusive workplace.

Chapter 5

Case Studies Overview

Case studies refer to in-depth investigations of a single entity, group, or situation. They are commonly used in academic, business, and medical research to provide detailed descriptions of real-life scenarios and to analyze the underlying factors that influence them. Case studies typically involve the collection of data from multiple sources, including interviews, observations, documents, and other forms of evidence.

In business, case studies are often used to analyze a particular company's success or failure in a specific market, while in medicine, they may be used to examine the causes and effects of a particular disease or treatment. In education, case studies are used to explore and understand a particular phenomenon or issue within a specific context, while in social sciences, case studies can help researchers to understand complex social interactions and dynamics. Overall, case studies are a valuable research tool that can provide deep insights into complex issues and help to generate new knowledge and understanding.

Examples of countries that have experienced a money crunch

There have been several countries that have experienced a money crunch or financial crisis in recent history. Here are a few examples:

Greece: In 2010, Greece faced a severe financial crisis due to high levels of government debt and deficits. The country's economy contracted, unemployment soared, and the government had to implement austerity measures to secure financial assistance from the International Monetary Fund and the European Union.

Argentina: Argentina experienced a major financial crisis in 2001-2002, which led to the largest sovereign default in history at the time. The country's currency collapsed, and many banks and businesses failed, leading to high levels of poverty and social unrest.

Venezuela: Venezuela has been facing a severe economic crisis since 2013 due to a combination of factors, including low oil prices, high levels of government debt, and hyperinflation. The crisis has led to shortages of basic goods and services, widespread poverty, and social unrest.

Zimbabwe: Zimbabwe experienced a severe economic crisis in the 2000s due to a combination of factors, including hyperinflation, corruption, and political instability. The country's currency became virtually worthless, and the government was forced to adopt foreign currencies as legal tender.

These are just a few examples of countries that have experienced a money crunch or financial crisis in recent history. Financial crises can have significant and long-lasting impacts on a country's economy and society, making it important for policymakers to take steps to prevent or mitigate them.

Chapter 6

Summary

Causes of Money Crunch

Summary of key factors that cause a money crunch

A money crunch, also known as a cash flow crisis or liquidity crisis, occurs when a business or individual experiences a shortage of cash to meet immediate financial obligations. Some key factors that can cause a money crunch include:

Poor financial planning: Failing to budget and plan for future expenses can result in a lack of available funds when unexpected expenses arise.

Slow-paying customers: If customers fail to pay their bills on time, it can create a gap between when a business incurs expenses and when it receives payment.

Over-investment: Investing too much capital in long-term projects or assets can leave a business short on cash in the short-term.

Economic downturns: Recessions and other economic downturns can lead to decreased revenues and increased expenses, making it difficult to meet financial obligations.

Over-reliance on credit: Relying too heavily on credit to finance operations can create a debt burden that becomes difficult to manage.

Seasonal fluctuations: Businesses that experience seasonal fluctuations in demand may struggle to generate consistent cash flow throughout the year.

Operational inefficiencies: Inefficient processes and high overhead costs can eat into profits and leave a business struggling to cover expenses.

Overall, it's important to have a solid financial plan and be aware of potential risks to avoid a money crunch.

recommendations for policymakers and individuals to prevent or mitigate a money crunch.

A "money crunch" can refer to a situation where individuals or organizations experience a shortage of funds or face financial difficulties. Here are some recommendations for policymakers and individuals to prevent or mitigate a money crunch:

For policymakers:

Ensure the availability of credit: Policymakers should work to maintain the availability of credit to individuals and businesses, particularly during economic downturns. This can be done by implementing policies that encourage lending, such as low interest rates or loan guarantees.

Foster a stable and growing economy: A stable and growing economy is essential for individuals and businesses to thrive. Policymakers should implement policies that promote economic growth, such as investing in infrastructure or supporting small businesses.

Provide safety nets: Policymakers can provide safety nets such as unemployment insurance or social welfare programs to help individuals and families weather financial difficulties.

Regulate the financial industry: Policymakers can regulate the financial industry to prevent fraud and other unethical practices that can lead to financial crises.

For individuals:

Establish a budget: Individuals should establish a budget to manage their income and expenses. This can help them to identify areas where they can cut back on spending and increase their savings.

Build an emergency fund: Having an emergency fund can provide a safety net in case of unexpected expenses or income loss. Individuals should aim to save at least three to six months' worth of living expenses in an easily accessible account.

Avoid debt: Avoiding debt or keeping it to a minimum can help individuals avoid financial difficulties. If debt is necessary, individuals should aim to pay it off as soon as possible to avoid accruing interest and other fees.

Invest in education and skills development: Investing in education and skills development can increase an individual's earning potential and job security, reducing the risk of financial difficulties.

Seek financial advice: Seeking the advice of a financial professional can help individuals to make informed decisions about their finances and plan for the future.

www.ingramcontent.com/pod-product-compliance
Lightning Source LLC
Chambersburg PA
CBHW071146220526

45467CB00015B/2040